Acknowledgment: For Tiana, my husband Mike, Sheldon, Marcia and Maben, as well as my dear friend Karen Cody for all your encouragement, love and support.

Text copyright ©2019 by Andreja Irving Semecnik
Illustrations copyright ©2019 by Nikola Pavlovic

All rights reserved. No part of this book may be reproduced, transmitted, copied, or stored in an information retrieval system in any form or by any means, graphic, electronic, or mechanical, including photocopying, taping and recording, without prior written permission from the publisher.

First edition 2019

Cataloguing in Publication Data
Irving, Andreja 1964-
Scoot To Bed

ISBN 978-1-9994057-0-0
9 8 7 6 5 4 3 2 1
First published by
Shadow Skyland Press
Surrey, British Columbia, CANADA

Scoot To Bed

Story by Andreja Irving Semecnik
Art by Nikola Pavlovic

The evening has come.

Tiana finished eating her dinner

and her mom finished cleaning

the dishes and the kitchen.

Soft shadows were falling into the room

from the windows.

Tiana's eyes were getting tired.

She let out a big yawn.

"It's time to scoot to bed, Tiana,"

said her mom.

"Go and...

brush your teeth

wash your face

"But I'm not tired, mommy.

Can I have a bedtime snack?"

asked Tiana.

"Of course", said her mom.

"But then right after that

go and...

brush your teeth

wash your face

"But I'm not tired, mommy.

Can I have a bedtime drink?"

pleaded Tiana.

"Here", said her mom.

"Take it to your room,

then...

brush your teeth

wash your face

"But I'm not tired, mommy.

Will you read me a story?"

"Sure," said her mom.

"Right after you...

brush your teeth

wash your face

"But I'm not tired, mommy.

Can you lay with me

while you read me a story?"

"Maybe", said her mom.

"Did you...

brush your teeth

wash your face

Ok then. Move over!"

said her mom and started to read

a great princess book:

"Once upon a time...."

"...The end."

"Mommy, since I

like you told me to,

can you read me another story?

Pleeeaasse!"

"Sure," said her mom

and picked up a wonderful big book with many pages.

"In the land far away, lived a curious little girl

...zzzzzz....,"

mom was asleep.

Tiana put her mom to bed. In Tiana's bed.

Tiana was happy.

But her mom did not

brush her teeth

wash her face

nor did she

get her pyjamas on

Very quietly, very carefully,

Tiana pulled up the covers,

snuggled up to mommy, smelled her scent,

listened to her even breathing,

closed her eyes and went to sleep.

And that was

Tiana's favourite bedtime routine.

THE END